Prese

_____

by

_____

on

_____

Mary Hears Good News

Matthew 1:18-21; Luke 1:26-56

God sent an angel to tell Mary good news! The angel surprised her. The angel said, "Don't be afraid, Mary! God has important news for you. You will have a baby. Name Him Jesus. He is the Savior God promised to send—God's own Son."

Mary wanted to TELL her good news! She went to see her cousin, Elizabeth. Elizabeth would soon have a baby, too! Elizabeth also knew that Mary's baby would be the Savior God promised to send. Elizabeth and Mary praised God together!

God sent an angel to another person. Joseph was going to be Mary's husband. In a dream, an angel talked to him.

Jesus is the most special baby ever born. He is God's Son.

The angel said, "Don't be afraid to get married to Mary. The baby is the Savior God promised to send. Name the baby Jesus." Joseph believed God's promise was about to come true!

Jesus Is Born

Luke 2:1-7

Mary's baby would be born SOON. Joseph told Mary, "We must go to Bethlehem, my home-town. We must write our names in the king's tax book."

Mary and Joseph packed their things. Mary
and Joseph walked and walked down the road
to Bethlehem. At night, they stopped and slept.
When morning came, they walked again!

Mary and Joseph got to Bethlehem at last.
The city was FULL of people. Joseph and
Mary needed a place to sleep. Joseph knocked
on the door of an inn. But there was no room.
It was full.

The innkeeper said, "Wait! You can use the stable!" Sheep, cows and donkeys slept there. But Joseph and Mary were glad for a place to rest!

That very night, in that very stable, Jesus was born. Mary wrapped Him up safe and warm.

God wants
everyone to
know about His
love. So He sent
Jesus to be
born.

She laid baby Jesus down in the
manger. He slept where the animals
eat. God's Son, Jesus, was born!

Shepherds and Angels

Luke 2:8-20

It was a quiet night. Stars twinkled high in the sky. Sheep and lambs lay sleeping together. Sleepy shepherds sat by their fire.

Suddenly, it was as bright as daytime! The shepherds looked up. An ANGEL! The angel said, "Don't be afraid! I have GOOD NEWS to tell everyone. In Bethlehem, JESUS, the Savior, is born! You'll find Him lying in a manger."

Then the whole SKY turned bright. It was filled
with angels! The angels praised God and said,
"GLORY TO GOD IN THE HIGHEST!"

Then the angels were gone. It was very quiet
and dark again. The shepherds looked at each
other. They said, "Let's go to Bethlehem and see
this BABY!" They hurried down the road!

The shepherds came to a stable. They could
see a newborn baby inside. He was lying in a
manger! They tiptoed in to see. Here was Jesus,
just as the angel had said! They were so happy!
They praised and thanked God.

Jesus brings good news to you and me. God loves us.

When the shepherds left the stable, they told everyone they saw, "Listen! We have good news! Jesus is born! GOOD NEWS!"

Wise Men Worship Jesus

Matthew 2:1-15

Jesus was born! God placed a bright new star in the sky. Far away, some wise men saw the star. They knew a great new King was born! They said, "Let's find this King. We'll bring gifts to Him!" So they loaded camels and began the trip.

They rode for days and days. One day, they reached Jerusalem. They went to King Herod's palace. They asked, "Where is the new King? We want to worship Him!"

King Herod wanted to be the ONLY king! Herod found out what God's Word said. It told where Jesus would be born. Herod told the wise men, "Go to Bethlehem. When you find the child, tell me so I can worship Him, too." But Herod really wanted to KILL Jesus!

The wise men followed the star to Bethlehem.
The star stopped over the place Jesus was!
The wise men got off their camels. They went
inside and bowed low. They gladly gave their
gifts. Here was Jesus, the King they had
followed the star to find!

The wise men MIGHT have gone back and told King Herod where Jesus was. But in a dream, God told them NOT to go back. They went home on a different road.

Then an angel told Joseph in a dream, "Get up! Take Mary and Jesus to Egypt. King Herod wants to hurt Jesus."

Mary and Joseph picked up Jesus. They traveled quietly and quickly. After many days, they were in Egypt! God kept Joseph and Mary and Jesus safe!

Jesus at the Temple

Luke 2:41-52

Baby Jesus grew and grew! He grew taller and
stronger and wiser. Joseph was a carpenter. He
made things out of wood. He taught Jesus how
to make things, too.

When Jesus was 12 years old, His family traveled to Jerusalem. It was a holiday! They went to the Temple to worship. They sang and prayed to God. They visited with relatives and friends.

After a week, they started walking home.
Everyone was busy talking and walking. They
walked all day. No one noticed that JESUS
wasn't there!

But when everyone stopped to sleep, Mary and Joseph looked for Jesus. They could not find Him anywhere! WHERE could Jesus BE?

Mary and Joseph hurried back to Jerusalem.
They looked EVERYWHERE for Him. They
looked all over the city for three days! Then
they went to search the Temple. They stopped,
amazed! THERE was Jesus!

You are growing taller and stronger and wiser. God takes care of you as you grow.

Jesus was talking to the Temple leaders! He wasn't afraid or sad. He was there to talk about God, His Father. He knew God was taking care of Him!